P9-DCH-027

This Journal Belongs to:

_____

ISBN 978-1-61626-042-2

Scripture quotations marked KJV are taken from the King James Version of the Bible.

Scripture quotations marked NIV are taken from the HOLY BIBLE, NEW INTERNATIONAL VERSION®. NIV®. Copyright © 1973, 1978, 1984 by International Bible Society. Used by permission of Zondervan. All rights reserved.

Scripture quotations marked NLT are taken from the *Holy Bible*, New Living Translation, copyright © 1996, 2004. Used by permission of Tyndale House Publishers, Inc., Wheaton, Illinois 60189, U.S.A. All rights reserved.

Scripture quotations marked NASB are taken from the New American Standard Bible, © 1960, 1962, 1963, 1968, 1971, 1972, 1973, 1975, 1977, 1995 by The Lockman Foundation. Used by permission.

Scripture quotations marked MSG are from *THE MESSAGE*. Copyright © by Eugene H. Peterson 1993, 1994, 1995, 1996, 2000, 2001, 2002. Used by permission of NavPress Publishing Group.

Scripture quotations marked ESV are taken from The Holy Bible, English Standard Version®, copyright © 2001 by Crossway Bibles, a publishing ministry of Good News Publishers. Used by permission. All rights reserved.

Scripture quotations marked NCV are taken from the New Century Version of the Bible, copyright © 2005 by Thomas Nelson, Inc. Used by permission.

Scripture quotations marked CEV are from the Contemporary English Version, Copyright © 1991, 1992, 1995 by American Bible Society. Used by permission.

Scripture quotations marked NKJV are taken from the New King James Version®. Copyright © 1982 by Thomas Nelson, Inc. Used by permission. All rights reserved.

Scripture quotations marked AMP are taken from the Amplified® Bible, © 1954, 1958, 1962, 1964, 1965, 1987 by The Lockman Foundation. Used by permission.

Published by Barbour Publishing, Inc., P.O. Box 719, Uhrichsville, Ohio 44683, www.barbourbooks.com.

Our mission is to publish and distribute inspirational products offering exceptional value and biblical encouragement to the masses.

Member of the
Evangelical Christian
Publishers Association

EVERYDAY

Joy

Journal

Janice Hanna

BARBOUR
PUBLISHING

Contents

Introduction

Everyday Joy

Is it really possible to have joy in your everyday life. . .even when the kids are crying and the bills are piling up? When you're overwhelmed with work or struggling with emotional problems? Can you truly "rejoice and be glad" in the midst of such trials? Of course you can! Joy is a choice, and it's one the Lord hopes you'll make in every situation. His joy will give you the strength you need to make it through. So, rejoice, dear one. Rejoice!

Anxiety

Know My Heart

Search me, O God,
and know my heart; test me
and know my anxious thoughts.

PSALM 139:23 NLT

Have you ever asked the Lord to give you an "anxiety check"?
He longs for you to live in peace, but that won't happen as long
as you're driven by worries and fears. Today, allow Him to
search your heart. Ask Him to dig deep. Are there cobwebs that
need to be swept out? Things hidden that should be revealed?
Let God wash away your anxieties, replacing them with His
exceeding great joy!

_____

_____

_____

_____

_____

_____

_____

_____

_____

_____

_____

Anxiety. . .a Joy Killer

Be anxious for nothing, but in everything by
prayer and supplication with thanksgiving let
your requests be made known to God.

PHILIPPIANS 4:6 NASB

$\mathcal{B}$e anxious for nothing? Is that possible? Aren't my anxieties
tied to my emotions? And aren't my emotions tied to the things
that happen to me? I can't control what happens to me, so how
can I control my reactions? Deep breath, friend! Instead of
knee-jerking when troubles come, slip into the throne room
and spend some time giving those problems to the Lord. With
thanksgiving, let your requests be made known to Him.

An Anxious Heart

A miserable heart means
a miserable life; a cheerful heart
fills the day with song.

PROVERBS 15:15 MSG

Have you ever felt weighted down? Heavy? Sometimes the cares of this life can make us so anxious that we only see the tips of our toes, not the road ahead. Today, lift your eyes! Speak words of faith and hope over your situation. Go out of your way to cheer someone else up. This simple act will lift your spirits and cause you to forget about your own burdens. Watch the joy sweep in!

Thou Shalt Not Worry!

"Do not worry about tomorrow, for tomorrow will worry
about itself. Each day has enough trouble of its own."

MATTHEW 6:34 NIV

What if the Lord had written an eleventh commandment:
"Thou shalt not worry"? In a sense, He did! He commands us
in various scriptures not to fret. So, cast your anxieties on the
Lord. Give them up! Let them go! Don't let worries zap your
strength and your joy. Today is a gift from the Lord. Don't
sacrifice it to fears and frustrations! Let them go. . .and watch
God work!

Anxious Striving

What does a man get for all the toil and anxious striving with which he labors under the sun?

ECCLESIASTES 2:22 NIV

Sometimes, out of anxiety, we bury ourselves in work. We labor from sunup till sundown. There's nothing wrong with working hard, but striving is another thing altogether. When we "strive," we're not trusting God to do His part. We're taking matters into our own hands. Today, take a moment to ask yourself an important question: "Am I working, or am I striving?" Don't let the enemy steal your joy! Strive no more!

....

....

....

....

....

....

....

....

....

....

Attitude

Attitude Equals Outcome

Serve the LORD with gladness: come
before his presence with singing.

PSALM 100:2 KJV

Attitude is everything. Our attitude determines our
outcome. We are challenged by scripture to serve with
gladness. (It's funny to think of *service* and *gladness* in the
same sentence, isn't it?) But here's the truth: If we serve with
an attitude of joy, it changes everything. Our service
doesn't feel like service anymore. It's a privilege!

Filled with Joy

And the disciples were filled with joy,
and with the Holy Ghost.

ACTS 13:52 KJV

$\mathcal{W}$ant to know the secret of walking in the fullness of joy? Draw near to the Lord. Allow His Spirit to fill you daily. Let Him whisper sweet nothings in your ear and woo you with His love. The Spirit of God is your comforter, your friend. He fills you to overflowing. Watch the joy flow!

....

....

....

....

....

....

....

....

....

....

Bubbling Joy

Can both fresh water and salt
water flow from the same spring?

JAMES 3:11 NIV

$\mathcal{C}$an you feel it. . .that bubbling in your midsection? Can you
sense it rising to the surface? Joy comes from the deepest
place inside us, so deep that we often forget it's there at all.
Wonder of wonders! It rises up, up, up to the surface and the
most delightful thing happens. Troubles vanish. Sorrows
disappear. Godly joy has the power to squelch negative
emotions. So, let the bubbling begin!

Joy. . .Minute by Minute

Keep your eyes focused on what
is right, and look straight
ahead to what is good.

PROVERBS 4:25 NCV

Ever wonder how you can be perfectly happy one minute and upset the next? If joy is a choice, then it's one you have to make. . .continually. We are often ruled by our emotions, which is why it's so important to stay focused, especially when you're having a tough day. Don't let frustration steal even sixty seconds from you. Instead, choose joy!

A Word in Due Season

**Everyone enjoys a fitting reply;
it is wonderful to say the right
thing at the right time!**

PROVERBS 15:23 NLT

 $\mathcal{E}$ ver had a friend approach you at just the right time—say, when you were really down—and speak something positive and uplifting? Ah, what perfect timing! You needed to hear something good, something pleasant. The right word at the right time was just what the doctor ordered, causing joy to spring up in your soul. The next time you see a friend going through a rough time, decide to speak that "good word."

Beauty for Ashes

Beauty for Ashes

To appoint unto them that mourn in Zion, to give unto them beauty for ashes, the oil of joy for mourning, the garment of praise for the spirit of heaviness. . .

ISAIAH 61:3 KJV

Seasons of mourning are difficult to bear, but praise God, He promises to give us beauty for ashes! He pours joy over us like a scented oil. . .to woo us out of periods of grieving. Can you feel it washing down on your head, even now? Can you sense the change in attitude? Slip on that garment of praise, believer! Shake off the ashes! Let God's joy overwhelm you!

_____

_____

_____

_____

_____

_____

_____

_____

_____

_____

The Oil of Joy

Let thy garments be always white;
and let thy head lack no ointment.

ECCLESIASTES 9:8 KJV

$\mathcal{W}$hat do the words "oil of joy" (Isaiah 61:3) mean to you? Can you envision the Lord anointing you with that precious oil? Do you feel it running over your head and down your cheeks? Oh, that we would always sense the joy of His anointing. That we would see ourselves as usable to the Kingdom. Today, as you enter your prayer time, allow the Lord to saturate you with His oil of joy.

19

The Garment of Praise

Awake, awake; put on thy strength,
O Zion; put on thy beautiful garments.

ISAIAH 52:1 KJV

*I*magine you've been invited to a grand celebration—perhaps
a wedding or a banquet. The clothes in your closet are old.
Boring. You need a new outfit, one worthy of such an occasion.
After serious shopping, you find the perfect dress! It's
exquisite, and when you wear it, you're in a party frame of
mind. That's what God desires from each of us. . .to "dress"
ourselves in garments of praise. It's time to party!

Lifting the Spirit of Heaviness

An anxious heart weighs a man down,
but a kind word cheers him up.

PROVERBS 12:25 NIV

Want to know how to get beyond a season of heaviness? Want to enter a season of joy? Speak uplifting, positive words. The things that come out of your mouth can make or break you. After all, we tend to believe what we hear. So, let words of joy flow. Speak hope. Speak life. And watch that spirit of heaviness take flight!

Shifting Sands

Let us hold unswervingly to the hope we profess,
for he who promised is faithful.

HEBREWS 10:23 NIV

*C*hange usually shakes us to the core. However, if you've been in a season of great suffering and you sense change is coming. . .you have reason to celebrate! The sands are shifting. The mourning is coming to an end. God, in His remarkable way, is reaching down with His fingertip and writing, "Look forward to tomorrow!" in the sand. Let the joy of that promise dwell in your heart. . .and bring you peace.

Betrayal

An Offering of Joy

Then my head will be exalted above the enemies who
surround me; at his tabernacle will I sacrifice with shouts
of joy; I will sing and make music to the LORD.

PSALM 27:6 NIV

It's one thing to offer a sacrifice of joy when things are going
your way and people are treating you fairly. But when you've
been through a terrible betrayal, it's often hard to recapture that
feeling of joy. As you face hurts and betrayals, remember that
God is the lifter of your head. Sing praises and continue to offer
a sacrifice of joy!

A Joyous Defense

But let all who take refuge in you be glad;
let them ever sing for joy. Spread your protection over
them, that those who love your name may rejoice in you.

PSALM 5:11 NIV

*O*h, the pain of betrayal. If you've been hurt by someone you trusted, choose to release that person today. Let it go. God is your defender. He's got your back. Take refuge in Him. And remember, praising Him—even in the storm—will shift your focus back where it belongs. Praise the Lord! He is our defense!

....

....

....

....

....

....

....

....

....

....

....

Hang On to Your Joy!

"The thief comes only to steal and kill and destroy; I have
come that they may have life, and have it to the full."

JOHN 10:10 NIV

*H*ave you ever been the victim of a robbery? It's a terrible
feeling, isn't it? Who would stoop so low? The enemy of your
soul is the ultimate thief. His goal? To steal from you. What is
he most interested in? Your peace of mind. Your joy. He often
uses betrayal as a mode of operation, so be wary! Next time
someone hurts you—or betrays you—don't let him or her steal
your joy. Stand firm!

Only Joy Remains

These things have I spoken unto you,
that my joy might remain in you,
and that your joy might be full.

JOHN 15:11 KJV

$\mathcal{W}$hen you've been badly hurt, it's hard to let go of the pain, isn't it? Sometimes it can crowd out everything—your peace of mind, your enthusiasm, your joy. If you're struggling with the effects of a betrayal today, don't allow it to consume you. Release it to God. Ask Him to replace the pain with His joy—a joy that will remain in you, never to be stolen again.

Come On. . .Get Happy!

But even if you should suffer for what is right, you are blessed. "Do not fear what they fear; do not be frightened."

1 PETER 3:14 NIV

It's one thing to suffer because of something you've done wrong; it's another to suffer for doing right. Even when we're unjustly persecuted, God wants us to respond in the right way. If you're suffering as a result of something you've done for the Lord. . .be happy! Keep a stiff upper lip! This, too, shall pass, and you *can* come through it with a joyful attitude.

Blessing

A Joyous Treasure

"The kingdom of heaven is like treasure hidden in a field.
When a man found it, he hid it again, and then in his joy
went and sold all he had and bought that field."

MATTHEW 13:44 NIV

*H*ave you ever stumbled across a rare treasure—one so
priceless that you would be willing to trade everything you
own to have it? If you've given your heart to Christ, if you've
accepted His work on Calvary, then you have already obtained
the greatest treasure of all. . .new life in Him. Oh, what
immeasurable joy comes from knowing He's placed that
treasure in your heart for all eternity!

_____

_____

_____

_____

_____

_____

_____

_____

_____

_____

_____

Extraordinary Blessing

There shall be showers of blessing.

EZEKIEL 34:26 KJV

*D*on't you enjoy walking through seasons of extraordinary blessing? We can hardly believe it when God's "more than enough" provision shines down upon us. What did we do to deserve it? Nothing! During such seasons, we can't forget to thank Him for the many ways He is moving in our lives. Our hearts must overflow with gratitude to a gracious and almighty God.

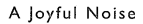

A Joyful Noise

Make a joyful noise unto the LORD,
all ye lands.

PSALM 100:1 KJV

How do we praise God for His many blessings? If we follow the pattern of Old Testament saints, then we lift our voices in thanksgiving! We let others know. With a resounding voice, we echo our praises, giving thanks for all He has done, and all He continues to do. So, praise Him today! Make a joyful noise!

Deep Joy

The LORD is my strength and my shield; my heart
trusts in him, and I am helped. My heart leaps
for joy and I will give thanks to him in song.

PSALM 28:7 NIV

Sometimes our sorrows run deep. We can feel buried alive.
That's why it's so important to allow our joys to run deep, too.
Today, as you ponder the many things you have to be thankful
for, pause a moment. Take a comforting breath. Thank God—
from the bottom of your heart—for the deep joys in your life.

Abounding with Blessings

A faithful man shall abound
with blessings.

PROVERBS 28:20 KJV

To abound means to have more than enough. When you're abounding, all your needs are met. . .and then some! How wonderful to go through such seasons. So, what do we have to do to qualify for these "more than enough" blessings? Only one thing. Be found faithful. Trust God during the lean seasons. Don't give up! Then, when the "abounding" seasons come, you can truly rejoice!

The Body Of Christ

Joy in Unity

Then make my joy complete by being like-minded,
having the same love, being one in spirit and purpose.

PHILIPPIANS 2:2 NIV

Want to know how to bring joy to God's heart? Live in unity with your Christian brothers and sisters. When we're like-minded, it pleases our heavenly Father. Are there problems to be ironed out with a Christian friend? Troubles in your church family? Let this be the day you fulfill His joy by resolving those differences. Let unity lead the way!

Infectious Joy

How lovely on the mountains are the feet
of him who brings good news, who announces
peace and brings good news of happiness.

ISAIAH 52:7 NASB

*E*ver had a contagious illness? Something like chicken pox
or measles? Maybe a bad cold? Surely you did your best *not* to
share it with your friends and co-workers. Joy is a lot like that.
It's contagious. You can spread it without even meaning to.
Pretty soon all your Christian brothers and sisters are catching
it. Now, that's one virus you don't need to worry about. . .so,
spread the joy!

Joyous Members

The body is a unit, though it is made up of many parts;
and though all its parts are many, they form one body.
So it is with Christ.

1 CORINTHIANS 12:12 NIV

$\mathcal{I}$t's fun to look around the church on any given Sunday
morning and see the various gifts at work. One teaches, the
other leads worship. One edifies, another handles the finances.
God didn't make us all alike. Praise Him for that! He recognizes
our differences. How do we merge all those unique people into
one body? We don't! That's God's job. We simply do our best to
remain unified members of a joyous family.

In the Midst of the Church

Saying, I will declare thy name unto my brethren,
in the midst of the church will I sing praise unto thee.

HEBREWS 2:12 KJV

The most amazing thing happens when we gather together in our various churches. When we lift our voices in joyous praise to the Lord, something majestic occurs. In the very midst of our praise, God declares Himself to His people. He's there! The next time you gather together with fellow believers for a time of worship, pause a moment, and reflect on the fact that you're entering into God's presence. . .together!

_____

_____

_____

_____

_____

_____

_____

_____

_____

_____

Joy in Serving

So we, being many, are one body in Christ,
and every one members one of another.

ROMANS 12:5 KJV

There's a lot of work to be done in the local church.
Someone has to teach the children, vacuum the floors, prepare
meals for the sick, and so forth. With so many needs, how
does the body of Christ function without its various members
feeling taken advantage of? If you're in a position of service
at your local church, praise God for the opportunity to serve
others. Step out. . .with joy leading the way.

Changing Seasons

A New Season

"A woman giving birth to a child has pain because her time
has come; but when her baby is born she forgets the anguish
because of her joy that a child is born into the world."

JOHN 16:21 NIV

If you've ever delivered a child, you know the pain associated
with childbirth. But that's not what you remember after the
fact, is it? No. As you hold that little one in your arms, only
one thing remains. . .the supernatural joy you experience as
you gaze into your newborn's eyes. The same is true with the
seasons we walk through. Sorrows will end, and joy will rise to
the surface once again!

Turn, Turn, Turn

To every thing there is a season, and a
time to every purpose under the heaven.

ECCLESIASTES 3:1 KJV

*O*h, those changing seasons! We watch in wonder as the
vibrant green leaves slowly morph into dry brown ones,
eventually losing their grip on the trees and drifting down to
the ground below. Change is never easy, particularly when you
have to let go of the past. But oh, the joy of recognizing that
God sees into the future. He knows that springtime is coming.
Our best days are ahead!

The Joy Set before Me

Let us fix our eyes on Jesus, the author and
perfecter of our faith, who for the joy set before
him endured the cross, scorning its shame, and sat
down at the right hand of the throne of God.

HEBREWS 12:2 NIV

Jesus walked through many seasons in His ministry here on earth. He walked through seasons of great favor, when crowds flocked to Him and when voices cried out, "Blessed is He who comes in the name of the Lord!" But He also walked through seasons of ultimate rejection as He headed up Golgotha's hill. We will go through good times and bad, but, like Jesus, we can say, "But for the joy set before me. . .I will endure."

Change Is around the Bend

" 'I will bless them and the places surrounding my hill.
I will send down showers in season; there will
be showers of blessing.' "

EZEKIEL 34:26 NIV

How do we shift from one project to the next? One phase of life to the next? We can move forward with joy leading the way when we realize that God is the giver of the seasons. He designed them and showers us with blessings as we move through each one, even the tough ones! Good news! Change is always just around the bend. Oh, the joy of knowing the hard times won't last.

Good News, Bad News

And they left the tomb quickly with fear and
great joy and ran to report it to His disciples.

MATTHEW 28:8 NASB

*E*ver had a day where all the news was good? You picked up
the phone. . .good news. Read an e-mail. . .good news. Then,
the very next day, all the news was bad! How do we make sense
of it all? Even those closest to Jesus went through ups and
downs. One moment they mourned His death. . .the next,
they celebrated His resurrection. Whether the news is good or
bad—choose joy.

Corporate Praise

Lift Up Your Voice!

And at midnight Paul and Silas prayed, and sang
praises unto God: and the prisoners heard them.

ACTS 16:25 KJV

Are you a closet praiser? Happy to worship God in the privacy of your own home but nervous about opening up and praising Him in public? Oh, may this be the day you break through that barrier. Corporate praise—coming together with your brothers and sisters in the Lord to worship Him—is powerful! May you come to know the fullness of His joy as you worship side by side with fellow believers!

A Song of Praise to Him

Let the children of Zion
be joyful in their King.

PSALM 149:2 KJV

Something about the voices of children lifted in joyous praise
does something to the heart, doesn't it? Innocent, trusting,
filled with pure happiness—their songs ring out for all to hear.
Can you imagine how God must feel when we, His children,
lift our voices, singing praise to Him? How it must warm His
heart! What joy we bring our Daddy God when we praise!

Praise Him in the Sanctuary

David also ordered the Levite leaders to appoint a choir of
Levites who were singers and musicians to sing joyful songs
to the accompaniment of harps, lyres, and cymbals.

I CHRONICLES 15:16 NLT

It's tough to lift up your voice when you're feeling down.
Sometimes you just don't feel like praising. However, coming
together as a team—a group—somehow boosts your strength!
Once those instruments begin to play and the first few words
of the songs are sung, you're suddenly energized as never
before. So, lift your voice with joy in the sanctuary!

Joy in the Battle

Then they returned, every man of Judah and
Jerusalem, and Jehoshaphat in the forefront of them,
to go again to Jerusalem with joy; for the LORD
had made them to rejoice over their enemies.

2 CHRONICLES 20:27 KJV

Enemy forces were just around the bend. Jehoshaphat, king of Judah, called his people together. After much prayer, he sent the worshippers (the Levites) to the front lines, singing joyful praises as they went. The battle was won! When you face your next battle, praise your way through it! Strength and joy will rise up within you! Prepare for victory!

_____

_____

_____

_____

_____

_____

_____

_____

_____

_____

_____

Joy. . .a Powerful Force

Praise ye the LORD. Praise God in his sanctuary:
praise him in the firmament of his power.

PSALM 150:1 KJV

There's just something amazing about being in a powerful worship service when all of God's children are like-minded, lifting up their voices in joyful chorus. The next time you're in such a service, pause a moment and listen. . .really listen. Can you sense the joy that sweeps across the room? The wonder? Oh, what a powerful force we are when we praise in one accord!

Disappointment

Rejoicing in the Hard Times

Yet I will rejoice in the LORD,
I will joy in the God of my salvation.

HABAKKUK 3:18 KJV

$\mathcal{P}$erhaps you've been waiting on pins and needles for something to happen—a promised promotion, an amazing opportunity, something wonderful. Instead, you get bad news. Things aren't going to pan out the way you expected. What do you do now? Instead of giving in to disappointment, continue to rejoice in the Lord and watch the disappointment lift. He will replace your sorrows with great joy.

....

....

....

....

....

....

....

....

....

....

....

A Glad Heart

A happy heart makes the face cheerful,
but heartache crushes the spirit.

PROVERBS 15:13 NIV

*H*ave you ever been so disappointed, so broken-down, that you felt you couldn't go on? Don't despair! Even in the hardest of times, it's possible to have a glad heart. The body reacts to the spirit, so if you want to keep on keepin' on, better do a heart check! No doubt, the cheerful expression on your face is sure to make others ask, "What's her secret?"

Disappointment. . .Be Gone!

And this hope will not lead to disappointment.

ROMANS 5:5 NLT

Tired of being disappointed time and time again? Ready for things to change? Try hope. Hope never leads to disappointment. When you're hopeful, you are anticipating good things, not bad. And even if the "good things" you're waiting on don't happen right away, you're energized with joy until they do. So, wave good-bye to disappointment. Choose hope. Choose joy.

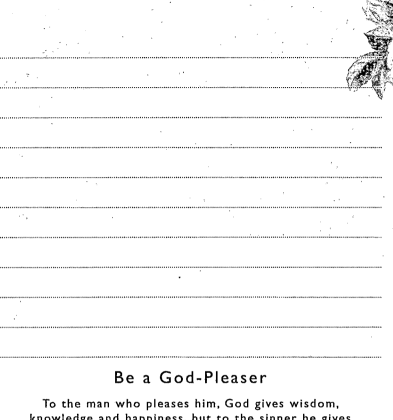

Be a God-Pleaser

To the man who pleases him, God gives wisdom,
knowledge and happiness, but to the sinner he gives
the task of gathering and storing up wealth to hand it
over to the one who pleases God. This too is
meaningless, a chasing after the wind.

ECCLESIASTES 2:26 NIV

Have you ever watched someone chase after fame, fortune,
or wealth? Maybe you've secretly longed for those same things.
Instead of chasing after the things this world can offer, which
are nothing more than wind, chase after God. Be a God-pleaser.
Store up *His* treasures. He is the giver of all things and will make
sure you have all you need. . .and more. What joy in finding that
treasure!

Rejoice. . .It's Worth Repeating!

Rejoice in the Lord always;
again I will say, rejoice!

PHILIPPIANS 4:4 NASB

Have you ever had to repeat yourself to a child, a spouse, or a co-worker? When we want to get our point across—or think someone's not listening as he or she should—we repeat our words. God knows what it's like! Some things are worth repeating, just because they're so good! "Rejoice in the Lord always: and again I say, Rejoice!" He tells us not just once, but twice. Better listen up!

_____

_____

_____

_____

_____

_____

_____

_____

_____

_____

_____

Eternity

Eternal Joy!

And the ransomed of the LORD shall return,
and come to Zion with songs and everlasting joy
upon their heads: they shall obtain joy and gladness,
and sorrow and sighing shall flee away.

ISAIAH 35:10 KJV

Have you ever pondered eternity? Forever and ever and
ever. . . ? Our finite minds can't grasp the concept, and yet one
thing we understand from scripture: We will enter eternity
in a state of everlasting joy and gladness. No more tears!
No sorrow! An eternal joy-fest awaits us! Now that's
something to celebrate!

Enter into the Joy

His lord said unto him, Well done, thou good and
faithful servant: thou hast been faithful over a few things,
I will make thee ruler over many things:
enter thou into the joy of thy lord.

MATTHEW 25:21 KJV

When you think of standing before the Lord—face-
to-face—are you overwhelmed with fear or awestruck with
great joy? Oh, what a glorious day it will be, when we hear
Him speak those words, "Well done, thou good and faithful
servant." When He ushers us into the joy of His presence for
all eternity, our fears and hesitations will be forever washed
away. Spend time in joyous rehearsal today!

54

The Joy of Heaven

I saw the LORD sitting upon his throne, and all the host of
heaven standing on his right hand and on his left.

2 CHRONICLES 18:18 KJV

What do you think of when you ponder the word *heaven*?
What will it be like to walk on streets of gold, to see our loved
ones who have gone before us? How thrilling to know we will
one day meet our Lord and Savior face-to-face. He has gone
to prepare a place for us—and what a place it will be! The joy of
eternity is ours as believers. Praise Him!

Joyous Heirs

That being justified by his grace,
we should be made heirs according
to the hope of eternal life.

TITUS 3:7 KJV

*H*ave you ever been the recipient of an inheritance? Ever had a family member pass away, leaving you money or objects? There is an inheritance that far exceeds anything we could ever receive in this world. By God's grace, we are His heirs! What do we inherit? Eternal life! If you haven't already done so, place your trust in Christ today, and experience the joy of becoming His child. Oh, the joy of a godly inheritance!

....

....

....

....

....

....

....

....

....

....

The Promise of Eternal Life

And this is what he promised us—even eternal life.

1 JOHN 2:25 NIV

$\mathcal{E}$ver had a friend or loved one make a promise, only to break it? What about you? Ever broken a promise? We all fail in this area, don't we? Thankfully, God is not a promise breaker. When He promised you would spend eternity with Him if you accepted the work of His Son on the cross. . .He meant it. Doesn't it bring joy to your heart to know God won't break His promises?

Family

Joy in the Family

Now the God of hope fill you with all joy and
peace in believing, that ye may abound in hope,
through the power of the Holy Ghost.

ROMANS 15:13 KJV

Living in a family environment isn't always easy. Siblings
bicker. Tempers flare. People get their feelings hurt. If you want
to experience joy in your family, then ask the Lord to give you
hope, especially when things are going wrong. Through the
power of the Holy Spirit, you can overcome those obstacles,
but you have to address them head-on. Today, make a list of
problems you're facing, then ask for God's input.

The Fruit of the Spirit

But the fruit of the Spirit is love, joy, peace,
longsuffering, gentleness, goodness, faith.

GALATIANS 5:22 KJV

*W*ant to know how to have the ideal family environment? Want to see parents living in peace with the teens, and vice versa? To obtain a joyous family environment, you've got to have a fruit-bowl mentality. Dealing with anger? Reach inside the bowl for peace. Struggling with impatience? Grab a slice of long-suffering. Having a problem with depression? Reach for joy. Keep that fruit bowl close by! It's going to come in handy!

No Greater Joy

I have no greater joy than to hear that
my children are walking in the truth.

3 JOHN 1:4 NIV

$\mathcal{G}$od rejoices in a strong family. To maintain healthiness, it's important to examine where you all stand—as individuals—in your relationship with the Lord. Sometimes we focus on our own spiritual lives but don't pay much attention to where our children are. Today, ask the Lord to show you what you can do to help your children grow in the Lord. As they grow. . .so will your joy. And so will the Lord's!

Open the Windows!

And there you shall eat before the LORD your God,
and you shall rejoice in all to which you have put
your hand, you and your households, in which
the LORD your God has blessed you.

DEUTERONOMY 12:7 NKJV

$\mathcal{D}$id you grow up in a family where laughter was a key
ingredient? Whether you grew up in a joyful home or not, it's
surely your desire for the family you now have (or may one day
have). God desires that your children walk in joy—and that
starts with you. Children are, after all, a reflection of their
parents. Today, throw open the windows of your home to
the possibility of everlasting joy!

Joyful Children

Let Israel rejoice in him that
made him: let the children of Zion
be joyful in their King.

PSALM 149:2 KJV

*O*h, the sound of children's joyful voices. It's like medicine for the sick. Balm for the weary soul. God longs for His children to rejoice in Him, to be joyful. And His desire for the family is no less. What would be the point of living in a home where everyone was sour and bitter? Today, ask the Lord to give every member of your household a fresh dose of His abiding joy.

Forgiveness

Joy in Forgiveness

Be kind to each other, tenderhearted, forgiving one
another, just as God through Christ has forgiven you.

EPHESIANS 4:32 NLT

Forgiveness is an interesting thing. When you release
from the sin he or she has committed against you,
ost like setting a bird free from a cage. You've freed
that person up to soar. And, in doing so, you've also freed
yourself up. No longer do you have to hold on to the bitterness
or anger. Letting go means you can truly move forward with
your life. . .in joy!

"Forgive Us Our Debts"

" 'Forgive us our debts,
as we also have forgiven our debtors.' "

MATTHEW 6:12 NIV

Is it true that God only forgives us to the extent that we forgive others? That's what the scripture teaches! It's so important not to hold a grudge. It hurts you, and it hurts the one you're refusing to forgive. If you've been holding someone in unforgiveness, may today be the day when you let it go. There is incredible joy—both in forgiving and *being* forgiven.

The Capacity to Forgive

Then Peter came to him and asked, "Lord, how often should I forgive someone who sins against me? Seven times?" "No, not seven times," Jesus replied, "but seventy times seven!"

MATTHEW 18:21–22 NLT

It's easy to get fed up with people who consistently hurt you and then ask for forgiveness. We grow weary with their promise that they won't do it again. If someone has repeatedly hurt you, ask the Lord to give you wisdom regarding the relationship, then ask Him to give you the capacity to forgive, even when it seems impossible. Surely joy will rise up in your soul as you watch God at work.

Friendship

Joyous Friendships

The sweet smell of perfume and oils is pleasant,
and so is good advice from a friend.

PROVERBS 27:9 NCV

$\mathcal{F}$riendship is a wonderful gift from God. A good friend leaves behind a "pleasant scent." And when you find a friend who offers wise counsel, you are doubly blessed! Today, don't just seek to *find* a friend like that; seek to *be* a friend like that. Leave behind a pleasant aroma to those God has placed in your life.

....

....

....

....

....

....

....

....

....

....

....

Dividing Joy

Tell this news with shouts of joy to the people;
spread it everywhere on earth.

ISAIAH 48:20 NCV

Joy is meant to be shared. (It's hard to keep to yourself, after all!) Think of it like a tasty apple pie. You can't eat the whole thing, can you? No, you need to spread the love, share the slices. So it is with joy. When you're going through a particularly joyful season, pass the plates. Sharing is half the fun!

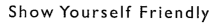

Show Yourself Friendly

A man that hath friends must shew himself friendly:
and there is a friend that sticketh closer than a brother.

PROVERBS 18:24 KJV

Ever met someone who just seems to have the gift of
friendship? She's a joy to be around and is always there when
you need her. Perhaps you're that kind of friend to others.
Friendship is a privilege, and we're blessed to have brothers
and sisters in Christ. But not all friendships are easy. Today,
ask the Lord to show you how to "show yourself friendly" in
every situation. Oh, the joy of great relationships!

_____

_____

_____

_____

_____

_____

_____

_____

_____

_____

_____

Greeting One Another in Joy

Speak to one another with psalms, hymns and spiritual
songs. Sing and make music in your heart to the Lord.

EPHESIANS 5:19 NIV

*W*ant to try a fun experiment? The next time someone asks
you how you're doing, instead of responding, "Okay," why not
get more specific? Try "I'm blessed!" or "Having an awesome
day!" Encourage yourself in the Lord, and He will keep those
spirits lifted. And encourage one another with words of
blessing, as well.

A Joyous Treasure

"I enjoyed your friendship so much.
Your love to me was wonderful."

2 SAMUEL 1:26 NCV

$\mathcal{I}$magine finding a trunk in your attic. You've never noticed it before. It's locked, but you manage to pry it open. Inside, to your great amazement, you find gold and silver coins. Hundreds of them! That treasure is no more special—no more amazing—than finding a friend. When you find a "kindred spirit," you've discovered a priceless treasure. Oh, the joy of a godly friendship!

Giving

A Receipt of Joy

"When I smiled at them, they could hardly believe it;
their faces lit up, their troubles took wing!"

JOB 29:24 MSG

Some folks are natural joy-givers! They thrive on bringing joy to others in their world. If that's your nature, then you need to know that God wants you to _receive_ joy, too. It's a dual process. When you give it, like a boomerang, it comes back to you! So, toss out some joy today. It will surely return, filling your heart and bringing a smile to your face!

Pressed Down, Running Over

Give, and it shall be given unto you; good measure,
pressed down, and shaken together, and running over,
shall men give into your bosom.

LUKE 6:38 KJV

Give, and it shall be given unto you." Likely, if you've been
walking with the Lord for any length of time, you've heard this
dozens of times. Do we give so that we can get? No, we give out
of a grateful heart, and the Lord—in His generosity—meets our
needs. Today, pause and thank Him for the many gifts He has
given you. Do you feel the joy running over?

....

....

....

....

....

....

....

....

....

....

....

_____

_____

_____

_____

_____

_____

_____

_____

_____

_____

_____

Giving Thanks

Let us continually offer the sacrifice of praise to God,
that is, the fruit of our lips, giving thanks to His name.

HEBREWS 13:15 NKJV

What do you think of when you hear the word *giving*?
Money? Gifts? Offerings? Time? Talents? Treasures? One of
the things we're called to give. . .is thanks! That's right. So,
pause a moment, and thank God for His many blessings in
your life. Feels good to give, doesn't it?

Giving Your Best

" 'You must present as the LORD's portion the best
and holiest part of everything given to you.' "

NUMBERS 18:29 NIV

Christians are called to give of their time, talents, and
treasures. Think about the time God has given you. What time
can you give back, and how? And what about your talents? Ask
the Lord to show you how to use them to advance the kingdom.
And your treasures? If you're struggling with giving to your
local church, make this the day you release your hold on your
finances. Give the Lord your very best.

_____

_____

_____

_____

_____

_____

_____

_____

_____

_____

_____

The Gift of Giving. . .in Secret

For they gave according to their means, as I can testify,
and beyond their means, of their own accord.

2 CORINTHIANS 8:3 ESV

Have you ever felt like giving, just to bless someone? Just
to bring joy to a friend's heart? Just to lift a burden? There's
something rather exciting about giving in secret, isn't there?
And when you reach way down deep—giving out of your own
need—it's even more fun. Today, take inventory of the people
in your life. Who can you bless. . .in secret?

God's Favor

Seasons of Favor

May those who delight in my vindication shout for joy and gladness; may they always say, "The LORD be exalted, who delights in the well-being of his servant."

PSALM 35:27 NIV

Do you ever feel like God's favorite child? Ever marvel at the fact that He continues to bestow His extraordinary favor upon you, even when you don't deserve it? God takes great pleasure in you and wants to bless you above all you could ask or think. So, when you're in a season of favor, praise Him. Shout for joy and be glad! Tell others about the great things the Lord has done.

78

Joy Comes in the Morning

For his anger lasts only a moment, but his favor
lasts a lifetime! Weeping may last through
the night, but joy comes with the morning.

PSALM 30:5 NLT

Can you picture a lifetime of blessing? Hard to imagine, isn't it? We think of "seasons" of blessing, but God continually pours out His favor upon His children. We have our ups and downs—our sorrows and our joys—but God remains consistent, never changing. We weep in the bad times and celebrate during the good. Oh, if only we could remember that on the tail end of every sorrow there is a joyful tomorrow!

Joyous Favor

May the favor of the Lord our God rest upon us;
establish the work of our hands for us—
yes, establish the work of our hands.

PSALM 90:17 NIV

It's interesting to think of "favor" and "the work of our
hands" in the same sentence, isn't it? In God's economy, favor
equals usefulness. We want the work of our hands to make a
difference in this world, and we want to see God smiling down
on our ventures. Today, ask God to establish the work of your
hands. Then watch as His favor rests upon you!

_____

_____

_____

_____

_____

_____

_____

_____

_____

_____

Finding Favor

But Noah found favor in the eyes of the LORD.

GENESIS 6:8 NIV

*E*ver wonder why Noah stood out head and shoulders above others in his generation? Why did God look upon him with favor? Noah walked with God and was righteous. Do you have what it takes to be a "Noah" in this generation? Walk with God daily. Don't let the things of this world zap your strength. Trust Him, live for Him, and watch Him rain down favor in your life!

Who Exalts?

No one from the east or the west or from the desert can exalt a man. But it is God who judges: He brings one down, he exalts another.

PSALM 75:6–7 NIV

Sometimes we grumble when others are exalted. We feel left out. Why do others prosper when everything around us seems to be falling apart? We can't celebrate their victories. We aren't joyful for them. Shame on us! God chooses who to exalt. . .and when. We can't pretend to know His thoughts. But we can submit to His will and celebrate with those who are walking through seasons of great favor.

....

....

....

....

....

....

....

....

....

....

....

God's Love

Amazing Love

He remembered his Covenant with them,
and, immense with love, took them by the hand.

PSALM 106:45 MSG

*Y*ou are loved. . .incredibly, sacrificially loved by the King of kings. Doesn't that fill you with overwhelming joy? Can you sense His heart for you? God's love is not based on anything you have done or will ever do. No. That amazing love was poured out on Calvary and beckons us daily. You are loved— today and always!

"For God So Loved. . ."

For God so loved the world, that he gave his only
begotten Son, that whosoever believeth in him
should not perish, but have everlasting life.

JOHN 3:16 KJV

The ultimate expression of love, one that will never be
surpassed, took place when God sent Jesus, His only Son,
to die on the cross for our sins. "For God so loved. . .that He
gave. . ." That's what love does. It gives and gives and gives.
Love is sacrifice—and in the person of Jesus Christ we witness
the ultimate sacrifice. Today, as you ponder God's love for
you, rejoice in the fact that He gave Himself willingly for you.

....

....

....

....

....

....

....

....

....

....

....

God Rejoices over Me

"The LORD your God is with you, he is mighty to save.
He will take great delight in you, he will quiet you with
his love, he will rejoice over you with singing."

ZEPHANIAH 3:17 NIV

It's fun to picture God celebrating over us, isn't it? Can you
imagine? He sings over us! He dances over us. He rejoices
over us! What joy floods our souls as we realize our Father
God, like a loving daddy, celebrates His love for His children.
Today, reflect on the thought that God—with great joy in His
voice—is singing over you.

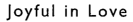

Joyful in Love

Keep yourselves in the love of God, looking for the
mercy of our Lord Jesus Christ unto eternal life.

JUDE 1:21 KJV

When you love the Lord and recognize His great love
for you, it's easy to be joyful! Think of His marvelous deeds.
Relish in His overwhelming love for His children. Recognize
His daily blessings. Oh, may we never forget that the Lord our
God longs for us to see the depth of His love for us. . .and to
love Him fully in return.

Love's Consolation

For we have great joy and
consolation in thy love.

PHILEMON 1:7 KJV

*H*ave you ever found yourself in need of consolation? Ever longed for someone to wrap his or her arms of love around you and make everything all right? God *is* that someone. We can take great consolation in His love, which is unchanging, everlasting, and abounding. Doesn't it bring joy to your heart to see how wide, how deep, and how long the Father's love is for His children?

God's Presence

Joy in His Presence

Splendor and majesty are before him;
strength and joy in his dwelling place.

1 CHRONICLES 16:27 NIV

In Old Testament days, only the high priest could enter the Holy of Holies to spend intimate time with God. However, when Jesus died on the cross, the veil in the temple was torn in two! We now have free access to the Holy of Holies, and Jesus bids us enter. . .often! He longs to spend time with us in that place. And oh, what joy, when we enter in! Make that choice today.

Make a Joyful Noise

Let us come before His presence with thanksgiving,
let us shout joyfully to Him with psalms.

PSALM 95:2 NASB

Sometimes we forget that the Lord loves us for to praise
joyfully. We get caught up in tradition, or maybe we just feel
uncomfortable worshipping with abandon. The Lord loves
a happy heart—and He truly enjoys it when we make a joyful
noise, lifting up our praises (our psalms) for all to hear. So,
break out of the box today! Be set free. . .to worship!

Fullness of Joy

You make known to me the path of life;
in your presence there is fullness of joy;
at your right hand are pleasures forevermore.

PSALM 16:11 ESV

When we stay on God's path—His road—we experience fullness in every area. And if we stick close to Him, which we are called to do, we will experience joy—not just now, in this life, but forevermore. Can you imagine. . .a joy that never ends? Draw near to the Lord. In His presence, you will find fullness of joy.

Joyous Refreshing

"Repent, then, and turn to God, so that your
sins may be wiped out, that times of
refreshing may come from the Lord."

ACTS 3:19 NIV

Think of a chalkboard, like the one your teacher used in
school. What if every bad thing you'd ever done was written
on the board? (Shivers!) Now envision the teacher taking the
eraser and blotting it all out. Wiping it away. As you watch
those sins disappear, you are flooded with joy. Your soul is
refreshed. The past no longer holds you back. Give your heart
to the Lord, and watch the refreshing come!

Dwelling in Joy

Surely the righteous will praise your
name and the upright will live before you.

PSALM 140:13 NIV

*H*ave you ever gone camping in a tent? What if you had a
special place—a quiet, private place like that tent—where you
could dwell with God? A private place of worship? Wouldn't
you want to linger inside that holy habitat, separating yourself
from the outside world? Pitch your tent today. . .and spend
some time inside with the King of kings.

_____

_____

_____

_____

_____

_____

_____

_____

Health Issues

Joyous Endurance

Behold, we count them happy which endure.
Ye have heard of the patience of Job. . .that the
Lord is very pitiful, and of tender mercy.

JAMES 5:11 KJV

It's interesting to think of the words *happy* and *endure*
in the same sentence. Twenty-first-century Christians are
accustomed to a fast-paced life, used to getting what they
want when they want it. But sometimes patience is required,
especially when we're not feeling well. Want to know the secret
of surviving the seasons that try your patience, the ones that
wear you to a frazzle? Endure! And happiness will prevail!

A Happy Heart

Therefore my heart is glad and my
glory [my inner self] rejoices; my body too
shall rest and confidently dwell in safety.

PSALM 16:9 AMP

*E*ver wish you could take a day off? Feel like you're always running full-steam ahead? The Lord designed our bodies to require rest, and if we skip that part of the equation, we suffer the consequences! If you want your body to "confidently dwell in safety," then you must get the rest you need. Rest makes for a happy heart. . .and a healthy body.

A Sacrifice of Praise

Is any among you afflicted? let him pray.
Is any merry? let him sing psalms.

JAMES 5:13 KJV

It's tough to praise when you're not feeling well, isn't it?
But that's exactly what God calls us to do. If you're struggling
today, reach way down deep. . . . Out of your pain, your
weakness, offer God a sacrifice of praise. Spend serious time
in prayer. Lift up a song of joy—even if it's a weak song! You'll
be surprised how He energizes you with His great joy!

Be of Good Cheer

A cheerful disposition is good for your health;
gloom and doom leave you bone-tired.

PROVERBS 17:22 MSG

$\mathcal{W}$ant to stay in the best possible health? Do you take vitamins every day? Eat right? Exercise? Here's one more thing you can add to your daily regimen for good health—a prescription for long life: cheerfulness. Yes, that's right! To ward off disease, try joy. According to the proverb above, it's the very flower of health. And it's just what the doctor ordered.

The Prayer of Faith

And the prayer of faith shall save the sick,
and the Lord shall raise him up.

JAMES 5:15 KJV

Have you ever wondered why God instructed church leaders to pray for the sick? Perhaps it's because, when we're sick, we often don't have the strength to pray for ourselves. We need our brothers and sisters in the Lord to cry out on our behalf. If you're struggling with illness, call for your Christian friends or church leaders to come and pray with you. What joy. . .when healing comes!

Hope

Joyous Hope

May the God of hope fill you with all joy and peace
as you trust in him, so that you may overflow
with hope by the power of the Holy Spirit.

ROMANS 15:13 NIV

Isn't it fun to think about God pouring joy into our lives?
Imagine yourself with a water pitcher in hand, pouring out,
out, out. . .covering everything in sight. The Lord wants us,
through the power of the Spirit, to overflow. To bubble over.
To experience not just joy, but hope—a benefit of joy. Today, as
you spend time in prayer, allow God to saturate you with His
joyous hope.

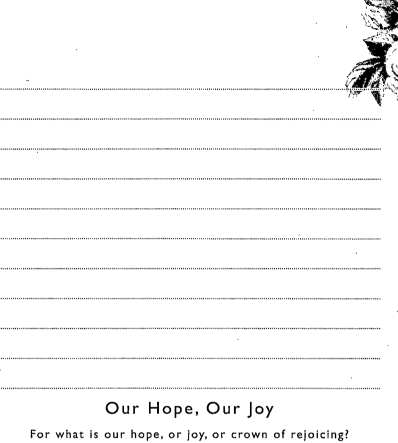

....

....

....

....

....

....

....

....

....

....

....

Our Hope, Our Joy

For what is our hope, or joy, or crown of rejoicing?
Is it not even you in the presence of our
Lord Jesus Christ at His coming?

1 THESSALONIANS 2:19 NKJV

Isn't it funny how the words *hope* and *joy* just seem to fit together? You rarely find one without the other. If you have hope in the unseen tomorrow, then joy rises up in your soul to give you strength for the journey. Spend time in God's holy presence today. In that place, you will find both hope. . .and joy.

Childlike Hope

For you have been my hope,
O Sovereign LORD, my
confidence since my youth.

PSALM 71:5 NIV

*R*emember how, as a child, you waited on pins and needles for Christmas to come? You hoped against hope you would get those toys you asked for. You knew in your knower that good things were coming. That same level of expectation can motivate you as an adult. Your Father wants you to trust Him with childlike faith. Put your trust in Him. . .and watch how He moves on your behalf.

Joyous Perspective

Let us draw near to God with a
sincere heart in full assurance of faith.

HEBREWS 10:22 NIV

*E*ver looked through a pair of binoculars? What if you peered through the lenses and caught a glimpse of God's face? What if you could see things the way He sees them? Hear things the way He hears them? What an amazing perspective! Every time you draw near to God, He offers you the opportunity to see Him. To find Him. To trust Him. Let Him give you His joyous perspective today.

Unexpected Joy

Do not be conformed to this world,
but be transformed by the renewing of your mind.

ROMANS 12:2 NKJV

$\mathcal{D}$o you ever find yourself worrying about tomorrow? Not sure of what it will bring? Oh, what hope lies in the unseen tomorrow! What unexpected joys are just around the corner. Sure, you can't see them. . .but they're there! Before you give in to fear, allow the Lord to transform your mind. See tomorrow as He sees it—filled with unexpected joys.

....

....

....

....

....

....

....

....

....

....

Impossible Situations

Joy. . .in Spite of. . .

"Until now you have not asked for anything in my name.
Ask and you will receive, and your joy will be complete."

JOHN 16:24 NIV

Have you ever faced a truly impossible situation? One so extreme that, unless God moved, everything else would surely crumble? God is a God of the impossible. And He wants us to ask, even when we're facing insurmountable obstacles. In fact, He wants us to know that only He can perform miracles. Our job? We're called to trust Him. Then, when those impossible situations turn around, our "joy tank" will be completely filled to overflowing!

I *Will* Rejoice!

This is the day the LORD has made;
let us rejoice and be glad in it.

PSALM 118:24 NIV

Are you having a hard day? Facing mounting problems? Maybe the bill collectors are calling, or the kids are sick. You're at the end of your rope. Pause for a moment and remember: *This is the day which the Lord has brought about. I will rejoice.* It's His day, and He longs for you to spend time with Him. Rejoice! It's the right choice.

Brought Forth with Joy

And he brought forth his people with joy,
and his chosen with gladness.

PSALM 105:43 KJV

Have you ever been delivered out of a terrible situation?
Lifted out of it, unharmed? Were you stunned when it
happened? Had you given up? God is in the deliverance
business! And when He lifts us out of impossible situations,
we are overwhelmed with joy. . .and we're surprised! Why do
we doubt His goodness? The next time you're in a tough spot,
expect to be "brought forth with joy."

The Joy of the Lord
Is Your Strength

"This day is sacred to our Lord. Do not grieve,
for the joy of the LORD is your strength."

NEHEMIAH 8:10 NIV

Is it possible to have joy in the middle of catastrophic
circumstances? What if you're facing the loss of a job? A
devastating illness? The death of a loved one? Can you really
look beyond your grief to find the joy? Our very strength comes
from the joy God places inside us, and we need that strength
even more when we're facing seemingly impossible odds!
Today, may God's joy strengthen you from the inside out.

Exceeding Joy

But rejoice, inasmuch as ye are partakers of Christ's
sufferings; that, when his glory shall be revealed,
ye may be glad also with exceeding joy.

1 Peter 4:13 KJV

$\mathcal{W}$e want to know Christ—both in the glory of His
resurrection and in the fellowship of His sufferings. If we're
open to really knowing Him in both ways, then we've got to be
vulnerable. Finding a balance is key. It really is possible to go
through times of suffering and still maintain your joy. After
all, joy is a choice.

Individual Praise

Make a Joyful Noise

O come, let us sing unto the LORD:
let us make a joyful noise to
the rock of our salvation.

PSALM 95:1 KJV

$\mathcal{D}$o you love to sing praises to God? Perhaps your voice isn't the best. Maybe you can't carry a tune in a bucket, but you long to praise God anyway. Go ahead and do it! We're told in scripture to "make a joyful noise" to the Lord. We're not told it has to be with a trained voice. So, lift up those praises! He accepts them, on key or off!

A Chorus of Praise

Sing for joy to God our strength;
shout aloud to the God of Jacob!

PSALM 81:1 NIV

Imagine you're in a room filled with noisy, fussy, crying
children. The combination of their voices raised in
miserable chorus is overwhelming. Now imagine that same
group of children, singing praise to God in unison. They're
making a joyful noise—and what a pleasant sound it is! Today,
as you face life's many challenges, focus on being a praise-
giver, not a fussy child.

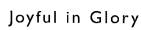

Joyful in Glory

Let the saints be joyful in glory:
let them sing aloud upon their beds.

PSALM 149:5 KJV

When do you like to spend time alone with the Lord? In the morning, as the stillness of the day sweeps over you? At night, when you rest your head upon the pillow? Start your conversation with praise. Let your favorite worship song or hymn pour forth! Tell Him how blessed you are to be His child. This private praise time will strengthen you and will fill your heart with joy!

With Thanksgiving

I will praise the name of God with a song,
and will magnify him with thanksgiving.

PSALM 69:30 KJV

It's one thing to spend time with God; it's another to praise Him with a thankful heart. Sometimes we forget His many blessings. We praise out of routine. Today, allow God to remind you of all the many ways He has blessed you. Oh, what full and thankful hearts we have when we pause to remember. Now, watch your praises rise to the surface, like cream to the top of the pitcher.

A Big Song

Shout for joy to the LORD, all the earth,
burst into jubilant song with music.

PSALM 98:4 NIV

$\mathcal{D}$o you ever feel like you don't have enough words to praise God? Like your vocabulary is limited? Wish you could throw the lid off and worship Him with abandon? That's exactly what He longs to do—spend intimate time with you. Sing a big song to the Lord. And prepare yourself for the inevitable joy that will rise up as you do.

....

....

....

....

....

....

....

....

....

....

The Journey

The Joyful Sound

Blessed is the people that know the joyful sound:
they shall walk, O LORD, in the light of thy countenance.

PSALM 89:15 KJV

Imagine a dimly lit room. You can barely make out the shapes
of things around you. Somewhere in that room, your Father is
waiting for you. Suddenly His voice rings out and joyous
relief floods your soul. Even though you cannot see where you
are going, the sound of His voice guides you directly into
His arms. Allow yourself to tune in to that precious
voice today.

Satisfied by Joy

Satisfy us in the morning with your unfailing love,
that we may sing for joy and be glad all our days.

PSALM 90:14 NIV

You've heard the adage, "You're only as old as you feel." One thing that ages us too quickly is discouragement. We get down, and it's hard to get back up again. We need to make a conscious effort each morning to reach out to God. . .to ask Him to satisfy us with His mercy, His loving-kindness. If we're truly satisfied, joy will come. And joy is the best antiwrinkle cream on the market.

....

....

....

....

....

....

....

....

....

....

....

Joy in the Journey

I press toward the mark for the prize
of the high calling of God in Christ Jesus.

PHILIPPIANS 3:14 KJV

Ever feel like the journey's too long? Like you're not making
progress? Today, ask the Lord to give you joy as you make your
way toward the goal. Don't fret if things aren't happening
as quickly as you want them to. Keep on pressing toward the
mark. Thank Him for the process, and take time to truly take
"joy in the journey."

Finishing with Joy

But none of these things move me,
neither count I my life dear unto myself,
so that I might finish my course with joy.

ACTS 20:24 KJV

The Christian life is a journey, isn't it? We move from point *A* to point *B*, and then on from there—all the while growing in our faith. Instead of focusing on the ups and downs of the journey, we should be looking ahead to the finish line. We want to be people who finish well. Today, set your sights on that unseen line that lies ahead. What joy will come when you cross it!

_____

_____

_____

_____

_____

_____

_____

_____

_____

_____

The Joy of His Heart

For he shall not much remember the days of his life;
because God answereth him in the joy of his heart.

ECCLESIASTES 5:20 KJV

Sometimes we go through things that we wish we could forget. Hard things. Hurtful things. But God, in His remarkable way, eases the pain of our bumps in the road, and before long, we can barely remember them. Joy rises up in place of pain, and we move forward, content in the fact that tomorrow will be better than yesterday. Don't focus on yesterday. Live for today and look forward to tomorrow.

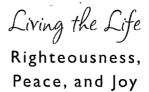

Living the Life

Righteousness, Peace, and Joy

For the kingdom of God is not meat and drink; but righteousness, and peace, and joy in the Holy Ghost.

ROMANS 14:17 KJV

Sometimes life can be drudgery. We wake up in the morning. Get dressed. Go to work (or stay home to care for our children). We drag home in the evening, spend a little time with our loved ones, then drop into bed, exhausted. Oh, there's so much more to life! The Lord wants to remind you that He has given you righteousness, peace, and joy. . .for every day of your life! So, celebrate!

Everyday Joy

For in him we live, and move,
and have our being.

Acts 17:28 KJV

Every breath we breathe comes from God. Every step we take
is a gift from our Creator. We can do nothing apart from Him.
In the same sense, every joy, every sorrow. . .God goes through
each one with us. His heart is for us. We can experience joy in
our everyday lives, even when things aren't going our way. We
simply have to remember that He is in control. We have our
being. . .in Him!

A Life of Joy

You have greatly encouraged me and
made me happy despite all our troubles.

2 CORINTHIANS 7:4 NLT

$\mathcal{W}$ant to know the perfect recipe for happiness? Spend your days focused on making others happy. If you shift your focus from yourself to others, you accomplish two things: You put others first, and you're always looking for ways to make others smile. There's something about spreading joy that satisfies the soul.

....

....

....

....

....

....

....

....

....

....

....

....

....

....

....

....

....

....

....

....

....

....

The Ways of Life

" 'You have made known to me the paths of life;
you will fill me with joy in your presence.' "

ACTS 2:28 NIV

$\mathcal{G}$od gives us everything we need to make it through life. He
teaches us His ways. Fills us with His joy. Gives us the pleasure
of meeting with Him for times of intimate worship. What an
awesome teacher and friend. He takes us by the hand and
gently leads us. . .from experience to experience. . .joy to joy.

Christis Lives in Me

I am crucified with Christ: nevertheless I live; yet not I, but Christ liveth in me.

GALATIANS 2:20 KJV

$\mathcal{W}$hen you gave your heart to Christ, the old you—the person you used to be—died. She's no longer alive. In a symbolic sense, you rose up out of that experience with God as a new creature—never again the same. So, the life you now live isn't really your own. It's His! And He lives in you. What a joyful exchange!

Mercy

Blessings on the Merciful

"Blessed are the merciful,
for they shall obtain mercy."

MATTHEW 5:7 NKJV

In some ways, mercy is like forgiveness. God offers it to the same extent we're willing to give it to others. The more merciful we are toward those who wrong us, the more merciful God is to us. And blessings flow out of relationships that extend mercy. Want to experience true joy today? Give. . .and receive. . .mercy.

His Mercy Endures Forever

O give thanks unto the LORD;
for he is good: for his mercy
endureth for ever.

PSALM 136:1 KJV

*G*od's mercy endures forever. It never ends. What about *our* mercy? How long does it endure? Until our patience is tested? Until someone rubs us the wrong way? Until we're hurt or offended by a friend or co-worker? If God's mercy endures forever, we should strive to be merciful, too. After all, if the King of kings offers it repetitively, shouldn't we do so, as well? Today, extend mercy. . .and watch the joy flow!

Merciful Joy

It is a sin to hate your neighbor,
but being kind to the needy
brings happiness.

PROVERBS 14:21 NCV

$\mathcal{O}$ur loving heavenly Father is so merciful toward us, and He expects us to treat others with mercy, too. Did you realize that having mercy on those who are less fortunate than you can actually make you happy? It's true! Reach out to someone today—and watch the joy start to flow!

Mercy Multiplied

Mercy unto you, and peace,
and love, be multiplied.

JUDE 1:2 KJV

$\mathcal{H}$ave you ever done the math on God's mercy? If so, you've probably figured out that it just keeps multiplying itself out, over and over again. We mess up; He extends mercy. We mess up again; He pours out mercy once again. In the same way, peace, love, and joy are multiplied back to us. Praise the Lord! God's mathematics work in our favor.

Fresh Mercy

The faithful love of the LORD never ends!
His mercies never cease. Great is his faithfulness;
his mercies begin afresh each morning.

LAMENTATIONS 3:22–23 NLT

$\mathcal{D}$on't you love the newness of morning? The dew on the grass? The awakening of the sun? The quiet stillness of the day when you can spend time alone with the Lord in solitude? Oh, what joy rises in our souls as we realize that God's love and mercy are new every morning! Each day is a fresh start, a new chance. Grace washes over us afresh, like the morning dew. Great is His faithfulness!

The Nations

Joy on That Glorious Day

Yea, all kings shall fall down before him:
all nations shall serve him.

PSALM 72:11 KJV

There's coming a day when every knee will bow and every tongue confess that Jesus Christ is Lord. Does it seem impossible right now, in light of current world events? If only we could see things the way God does! He knows that the kings of the nations will one day fall down before Him. Oh, what a glorious and joyful day that will be!

Joy for the Nations

Therefore the redeemed of the LORD shall return,
and come with singing unto Zion; and everlasting joy shall
be upon their head: they shall obtain gladness and joy;
and sorrow and mourning shall flee away.

ISAIAH 51:11 KJV

God longs for people across the globe to turn their hearts
to Him. He wants them to understand that He sent His only
begotten Son to earth to die on a rugged cross so that people
of every race, creed, and color could be set free from their
sins. Oh, that people around the world would turn to God,
would return to Him with singing, and with everlasting
joy upon their heads!

Joy in the Cities

And there was great joy in that city.

ACTS 8:8 KJV

Can you imagine the church of Jesus Christ—alive and vibrant in *every* city around the world? Alive in Moscow. Alive in Paris. Alive in Havana. Alive. . .in your hometown. Oh, the celebration that will ensue when cities around the world are eternally changed. Today, choose a particular city and commit to pray for that place. . .that all might come to know Him!

Rejoicing Rulers

The king shall joy in thy strength, O LORD;
and in thy salvation how greatly shall he rejoice!

PSALM 21:1 KJV

$\mathcal{I}$t's so important to pray for our rulers. They need our
undergirding, our daily intercession, and our prayers for their
safety and wisdom. Today, as you contemplate your current
political leaders, pause a minute and lift their names up in
prayer. May they all find strength in the joy of the Lord. May
each come to the fullness of salvation. And may the people
rejoice as a result of what the Lord has done!

Praise Him, All You Nations!

All of you nations, come praise the LORD!
Let everyone praise him.

PSALM 117:1 CEV

$\mathcal{C}$an you imagine the sound of millions of people, singing praises to the Lord in thousands of different languages simultaneously? On any given day, God hears people all over the world lift up their praises to Him in their native tongues. Oh, what a joyful sound that must be to our heavenly Father. Today, as you lift your voice, think of the millions of others who join you. Praise Him! Oh, praise Him!

_____

_____

_____

_____

_____

_____

_____

_____

_____

_____

_____

_____

Nature

Nature's Joyous Song

Let the floods clap their hands:
let the hills be joyful together.

PSALM 98:8 KJV

All of nature sings the praises of our mighty God. Look around you! Do you see the hills off in the distance, pointing up in majesty? Can you hear the water in the brooks, tumbling along in a chorus of praise? And what about the ocean waves? Oh, the joy in discovering the God of the universe through His marvelous creation!

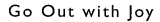

Go Out with Joy

For ye shall go out with joy, and be led forth with peace:
the mountains and the hills shall break forth before you into
singing, and all the trees of the field shall clap their hands.

ISAIAH 55:12 KJV

$\mathcal{G}$od reveals Himself in a million different ways, but perhaps the most breathtaking is through nature. The next time you're in a mountainous spot, pause and listen. Can you hear the sound of God's eternal song? Does joy radiate through your being? Aren't you filled with wonder and with peace? The Lord has, through the beauty of nature, given us a rare and glorious gift.

(blank lined writing space)

Sing, O Heavens!

Sing, O heavens; and be joyful, O earth; and break forth into singing, O mountains: for the LORD hath comforted his people, and will have mercy upon his afflicted.

ISAIAH 49:13 KJV

$\mathcal{I}$magine you're walking through a meadow on a dewy morning. The sweet smell of dawn lingers in the air. Suddenly, like a skilled orchestra, the heavens above begin to pour out an unexpected song of joy. You close your eyes, overwhelmed by the majesty of the moment. Scripture tells us the heavens and the earth are joyful. . .so tune in to their chorus today.

A Joy Forever

The Mighty One, God, the LORD, speaks and summons the earth from the rising of the sun to the place where it sets. From Zion, perfect in beauty, God shines forth.

PSALM 50:1–2 NIV

A child's face. A flowering pear tree. A rippling brook. A mountain's peak. All of these things overwhelm us with the magnitude of their beauty. Why? Because we can see that they were created by Someone much larger than ourselves—Someone incredibly creative and colorful. We are reminded of the awesomeness of God. Focus on the beauty He has placed in your world. . .and praise Him!

Nature's Joys

The heavens declare the glory of God;
the skies proclaim the work of his hands.

PSALM 19:1 NIV

*O*h, the wonder of God's creation! Who could paint the skies such a brilliant blue? And who could give such detail to such a tiny blade of grass? Only our creative Lord! Spend some time outdoors with Him today, soaking in the beauty of your surroundings. Allow the joy to permeate your soul, and give thanks to our awesome God, Creator of all.

New Beginnings

Second Chances

For his anger lasts only a moment; but his favor lasts a lifetime; weeping may remain for a night, but rejoicing comes in the morning.

PSALM 30:5 NIV

*D*on't you love second chances? New beginnings? If only we could go back and redo some of our past mistakes. . .what better choices we'd make the second time around. Life in Jesus is all about the rebirth experience—the opportunity to start over. Each day is a new day, in fact. And praise God! The sorrows and trials of yesterday are behind us. With each new morning, joy dawns!

....

....

....

....

....

....

....

....

....

Exceeding Great Joy

When they saw the star, they rejoiced
with exceeding great joy.

MATTHEW 2:10 KJV

$\mathcal{C}$an you imagine the wise men, gazing upon that star for the first time? Finally! The long-awaited day had come. What joy they must have felt in their hearts. Surely they could sense the beginning of a new era. The gospel message is all about new beginnings. We rejoice every time we're given a chance to begin again. Praise God for the many times He's given you a fresh start.

Out of the Pit

I waited patiently for the LORD. He turned to me and heard my cry. He lifted me out of the pit of destruction, out of the sticky mud. He stood me on a rock and made my feet steady.

PSALM 40:1–2 NCV

When you've been living in the pit, you can hardly imagine being lifted out of it. Oh, the joy of knowing God can bring us out of even the deepest, darkest pit and place our feet on solid ground. Nothing is impossible with our Lord! If you're in a dark place today, call out to Him. . .and watch as He delivers you. He will establish your steps. Praise Him!

....

....

....

....

....

....

....

....

....

....

On Wings of Joy

"All the earlier troubles, chaos, and pain are things
of the past, to be forgotten. Look ahead with joy.
Anticipate what I'm creating."

ISAIAH 65:17–18 MSG

We don't always get it right, do we? Sometimes we make mistakes. But our mistakes spur us on to begin again. We want to get it right the next time. And praise God! He gives us chance after chance, opportunity after opportunity. Let the joys of your past successes merge with the "spurs" of your past failings so that you can set out on a road of new beginnings.

The New Man

And have put on the new self, which is being
renewed in knowledge in the image of its Creator. . .

COLOSSIANS 3:10 NIV

Are there people in your life you've given up on? Maybe someone you've been praying for, for years? You're convinced he or she will never come to the Lord? Today, ponder the new beginnings in your own life. Hasn't God re-created you? Renewed you? Won't He do the same for others? Feel the joy rise up as you ponder the possibilities? Pray for that friend or loved one to "put on the new self."

Obedience

Joyful Obedience

Now unto him that is able to keep you from falling,
and to present you faultless before the presence
of his glory with exceeding joy. . .

JUDE 1:24 KJV

$\mathcal{O}$ur obedience makes God happy—and should make us happy, too. In fact, the more difficult it is to obey, the more joyful we should be. Why? Because a big situation calls for a big God. And our God is bigger than anything we could ask or think. He alone can prevent us from falling. So, if you're struggling in the area of obedience, surrender your will. Enter into joyful obedience.

Used for a Purpose

Become the kind of container God can
use to present any and every kind of gift
to his guests for their blessing.

2 TIMOTHY 2:21 MSG

Want to reach the end of your life feeling completely fulfilled? Want to know true joy? Then allow the Lord to use you. Does that idea contradict what you've been taught in this "me first" society? Being "used" by God is far different from being "used" by people. Being usable is our goal, our ambition. Today, offer your gifts and abilities to the Lord so that they can be used for His purpose and His glory.

Something to Talk About

Everyone has heard about your obedience, so I am full
of joy over you; but I want you to be wise about what is
good, and innocent about what is evil.

ROMANS 16:19 NIV

Ever been caught in a situation where people were talking
about you behind your back? Maybe folks you loved and
trusted? How did that make you feel? Well, how would you feel
if you found out people were talking about you. . .because of
your obedience? Wow! That's a different thing altogether. Let
them talk! May our joyful obedience to the Lord win us a spot
in many cheerful conversations!

145

Years of Pleasure

If they obey and serve him,
they shall spend their days in prosperity,
and their years in pleasures.

JOB 36:11 KJV

*I*f you knew that your disobedience was going to cost you dearly, would you be more inclined to obey? If you knew that your obedience would be rewarded, would that spur you on to do the right thing? Scripture convinces us that our days can be spent in prosperity and our years in pleasures if we will simply obey and serve the Lord. Oh, the joy of obedience!

....

....

....

....

....

....

....

....

....

....

....

Uprightness

"I know also, my God, that You test the
heart and have pleasure in uprightness."

1 CHRONICLES 29:17 NKJV

*E*veryone wants to be happy, right? We know that our
obedience to the Lord results in a life of great joy. But our
obedience does something else, too. It brings pleasure to our
heavenly Father. When we live uprightly, God is pleased. Today,
instead of focusing on your own happiness, give some thought
to putting a smile on *His* face.

Overflowing Joy

Limitless Joy

"I have told you this so that my joy may be
in you and that your joy may be complete."

JOHN 15:11 NIV

$\mathcal{D}$id you realize that joy is limitless? It knows no boundaries.
Jesus poured Himself out on the cross at Calvary—giving
everything—so that you could experience fullness of joy. Even
now, God longs to make Himself known to you in such a new
and unique way. May you burst at the seams with this limitless
joy as you enter His presence today.

Spilling Over

And these things write we unto you,
that your joy may be full.

1 JOHN 1:4 KJV

Imagine you're in the process of filling a glass with water and accidentally pour too much in. The excess goes running down the sides, splashing your hand and anything else it comes in contact with. That's how it is when you're overflowing with joy from the inside out. You can't help but spill out onto others, and before long, they're touched, too. So, let it flow!

I've Got the Joy!

I will greatly rejoice in the LORD,
my soul shall be joyful in my God.

ISAIAH 61:10 KJV

As children we used to sing, "I've got the joy, joy, joy, joy down in my heart!" We bounced up and down in our seats with great glee. Do you still have that joy? Has it lingered into your adulthood? Do you sense it to the point where you could come bounding from your chair, ready to share what He's given you with a lost and dying world? Oh, for such a childlike joy!

Shout for Joy!

Be glad in the LORD and rejoice, you righteous ones; and shout for joy, all you who are upright in heart.

PSALM 32:11 NASB

Have you ever been so happy that you just felt like shouting? Ever been so overcome with joy that you wanted to holler your praise from the rooftops for all to hear? Well, what's holding you back? Go for it! Shout for joy! Let the whole world hear your praises to the King of kings!

Joy-Scatterers

Light-seeds are planted in the souls
of God's people, joy-seeds are
planted in good heart-soil.

PSALM 97:11 MSG

*I*magine a farmer dropping seeds into fertile soil. They're sure to spring up. That's how it is with joy. Keep it with you at all times, like seeds in your pocket. Then, when you find fertile soil—in the workplace, at the doctor's office, around the dinner table—pull out a few of those seeds and sprinkle them around. Oh, the joy that will spring forth!

....

....

....

....

....

....

....

....

....

....

Patience

Joyful Patience

Strengthened with all might, according
to his glorious power, unto all patience
and longsuffering with joyfulness. . .

COLOSSIANS 1:11 KJV

*Y*ou've heard the old adage, "Don't pray for patience! God
will surely give you a reason to need it!" Here's the truth: As
you wait on the Lord, He promises to strengthen you with
all might, according to His glorious power. So, what's a little
waiting, as long as God is giving you strength? And you know
where that strength comes from after all. . .the joy of the Lord
is your strength!

Wanting Nothing

But let patience have its perfect work,
that you may be perfect and complete, lacking nothing.

JAMES 1:4 NKJV

$\mathcal{L}$et patience have its perfect work? Ouch! It's hard enough to wait, even harder to wait patiently. Now we're supposed to let patience "work" in us while we're waiting? Sounds painful . . .and nearly impossible! But when we allow patience to have its perfect work in us, we are "complete," wanting nothing. We can wait patiently. . .and not stress about the yet-unanswered prayers. Every need is met in Him. Talk about joy!

....

....

....

....

....

....

....

....

....

....

Rejoicing in Hope

[Be] rejoicing in hope; patient in tribulation;
continuing instant in prayer.

ROMANS 12:12 KJV

The words *rejoice* and *hope* just seem to go together, don't they? There's something about choosing joy that fills our hearts with hope for better days ahead. So what, if we have to wait awhile? If we stay focused on the Lord, casting our cares on Him, that day of rejoicing will surely come!

The Path of Joy

Moses spoke to the people: "Don't be afraid.
Stand firm and watch GOD do his work
of salvation for you today."

EXODUS 14:13 MSG

*W*hen we're waiting on a miracle, the minutes seem to drag by. We force our attentions ahead to tomorrow. . .in the hopes that we'll receive the answer we long for. But what about today? This is the day the Lord has made! He wants us to rejoice in it. So what if the answer hasn't come yet? So what if patience is required? Don't miss the opportunity to connect with God. . .today!

_____

_____

_____

_____

_____

_____

_____

_____

_____

_____

_____

Joyous Tomorrow

But if we hope for that we see not,
then do we with patience wait for it.

ROMANS 8:25 KJV

Are you in a "waiting" season? Is your patience being tested to the breaking point? Take heart! You are not alone. Every godly man and woman from biblical times till now went through seasons of waiting on the Lord. Their secret? They hoped for what they could not see. (They never lost their hope!) And they waited patiently. So, as you're waiting, reflect on the biblical giants and realize. . .you're not alone!

Prayer

Answered Prayers

> But the angel said to him, "Do not be afraid, Zacharias,
> for your prayer is heard; and your wife Elizabeth will
> bear you a son, and you shall call his name John."

LUKE 1:13 NKJV

Zacharias, though quite old, had been praying for a child for years. How funny that the angel prepared him by saying, "Don't be afraid," before sharing the news! This answered prayer, though joyous, surely rocked Zacharias and Elizabeth's world! Have you ever consistently prayed for something without getting the answer you want? Ever felt like giving up? Don't! When you least expect it, your answer could come. . . and it just might rock your world!

Approaching the Throne with Joy

In every prayer of mine I always make my entreaty
and petition for you all with joy (delight).

PHILIPPIANS 1:4 AMP

$\mathcal{S}$ometimes we approach our prayer time with God with a list in hand, much like a child at Christmastime. Other times, we approach the Lord with fear leading the way. "What happens if He doesn't respond like I hope?" Though we don't need to come with a Christmas list in hand, we do need to confidently approach our heavenly Father and make our requests with joy. He loves us, after all! So, draw near!

Continued Prayers

Continue in prayer, and watch
in the same with thanksgiving.

COLOSSIANS 4:2 KJV

Are you the sort of person who gives up easily? Does your faith waver if God doesn't respond to your prayers right away? Don't give up, and don't stop praying, particularly if you're believing God for something that seems impossible. Be like that little widow woman in the Bible. . .the one who pestered the judge until he responded. Just keep at it. As you continue in prayer, keep a joyful heart, filled with expectation.

Enjoying Life

Let all who seek You rejoice and be glad in You; and let those who love Your salvation say continually, "Let God be magnified." . . . You are my help and my deliverer.

PSALM 70:4–5 NASB

$\mathcal{S}$ometimes we approach God robotically: "Lord, please do this for me. Lord, please do that." We're convinced we'll be happy, if only God grants our wishes like a genie in a bottle. We're going about this backward! We should start by praising God. Thank Him for life, health, and the many answered prayers. Our joyous praise will remind us just how blessed we already are! Then—out of genuine relationship—we make our requests known.

Joy Leads the Way

Then will I go unto the altar of God,
unto God my exceeding joy: yea, upon the
harp will I praise thee, O God my God.

PSALM 43:4 KJV

We're instructed to come into the Lord's presence with a joy-filled heart. . .to praise our way into the throne room. Perhaps you're not a musician. You don't own an instrument and only sing in the shower. Don't let that keep you from approaching the altar with a song of praise on your lips. Today, let joy lead the way, and may your praises be glorious!

Provision

Daily Provision

"Who provides food for the raven when its young
cry out to God and wander about for lack of food?"

JOB 38:41 NIV

$\mathcal{D}$oes it fill your heart with joy to know that God provides for
your needs? He makes provision. . .both in seasons of want
and seasons of plenty. There's no need to strive. No need to
worry. He's got it all under control. If He provides food for the
ravens, then surely He knows how to give you everything you
need when you need it. So, praise Him!

Joyous Provision

And my God will meet all your needs according
to his glorious riches in Christ Jesus.

PHILIPPIANS 4:19 NIV

$\mathcal{S}$ometimes God goes overboard when it's time to make
provision. He blesses us above and beyond what we could ask
or think. He not only meets our needs. . .He throws in a bit of
excess, just to watch us smile. If you're in a season of abundant
provision, remember to share the joy! Pass on a portion of
what He has given you. And praise Him! What an awesome God
we serve!

....

....

....

....

....

....

....

....

....

....

Who Provides?

Consider the lilies how they grow:
they toil not, they spin not.

LUKE 12:27 KJV

Sometimes we look at our job as our provision. We say things like, "I work for my money." While it's true that we work hard (and are rewarded with a paycheck), we can't forget that God is our provider. If He cares for the lilies of the field—flowers that bloom for such a short season—then how much more does He care for us, His children? What joy. . .realizing God loves us enough to provide for our needs.

Joyfully Satisfied

"I will abundantly bless her provision;
I will satisfy her needy with bread."

PSALM 132:15 NASB

The Lord has promised to meet all our needs according to His riches in glory. His heart is for His people, especially the poor and downtrodden. Today, as you seek God about your own needs, ask Him how you can help meet the needs of the less fortunate in your community. What a joy it will be to reach out to others. . .even if you're also in need.

....

....

....

....

....

....

....

....

....

....

Hearts Filled with Joy

"He provides you with plenty of
food and fills your hearts with joy."

ACTS 14:17 NIV

*W*hen we think about provision, we usually think in terms
of money, don't we? Getting the bills paid. Having food in the
pantry. Making sure our needs are met. But what about our
emotional needs? Does the Lord make provision in that area,
as well? Of course! According to this scripture, He fills our
hearts with joy. What an awesome God we serve!

Salvation

Joy in Heaven

"In the same way, there is more joy in heaven over one lost
sinner who repents and returns to God than over ninety-
nine others who are righteous and haven't strayed away!"

LUKE 15:7 NLT

*W*hat a party heaven throws when one person comes to
know the Lord! Can't you see it now? The angels let out a
shout! The trumpeters play their victory chant. All of heaven
reacts joyfully to the news. Oh, that we would respond with
such joy to the news of a lost soul turning to the Lord. What a
celebration!

Rejoicing in Salvation

Then my soul will rejoice in the
LORD and delight in his salvation.

PSALM 35:9 NIV

*D*o you remember what it felt like to put your trust in Christ
for the first time? Likely, you've never experienced anything
else that brought such joy, such release. Oh, the joy of that
salvation experience. The overwhelming realization that the
God of the universe loves you—enough to send His only Son
to die on a cross so that you could have eternal life. There's no
greater joy than the joy of salvation.

Restored Joy

Restore unto me the joy of thy salvation;
and uphold me with thy free spirit.

PSALM 51:12 KJV

$\mathcal{W}$hen you restore your home, you return it to its prior state—its best possible condition. But is it possible to restore joy? Can you really get it back once lost? Of course you can! Joy is a choice and can be restored with a single decision. Decide today. Make up your mind. Get ready for the renovation to take place as you ask the Lord to restore the joy of your salvation.

Wells of Salvation

With joy you will drink deeply
from the fountain of salvation!

ISAIAH 12:3 NLT

In biblical times, women would go to the local well for water.
They would drop the bucket down, down, down, then lift it
up, filled to the brim. Today, the Lord wants you to reach
down into His well of salvation and, with great joy, draw up
the bucket. Remember how He saved you? Delivered you?
Remember His grace? Is your bucket filled to the brim? If so,
then that's something to celebrate!

The Rock of
Our Salvation

O come, let us sing unto the LORD:
let us make a joyful noise to the
rock of our salvation.

PSALM 95:1 KJV

God never changes. He's the same—yesterday, today, and forever. We go through a multitude of changes in our lives, but, praise God, He's consistent. Doesn't that bring joy to your heart, to realize that the Creator of the universe is our Rock? And don't you feel like celebrating when you realize that, no matter how much you mess up, His promise of salvation is true? Praise be to the Lord, our Rock!

Sorrow and Suffering

Joy in Place of Tears

They that sow in tears shall reap in joy.

PSALM 126:5 KJV

Periods of great sorrow are unavoidable. Perhaps the death of a loved one has left you floundering. Or maybe your heart has been broken by someone you thought you could trust. If you've been through an earthshaking change—one you weren't expecting or feel you didn't deserve—then turn to the One who can replenish you. God will walk with you through this valley and promises to replace your tears with joy.

173

A Compassionate Heart

Break forth into joy, sing together, you waste
places of Jerusalem! For the LORD has comforted
His people, He has redeemed Jerusalem.

ISAIAH 52:9 NKJV

Have you ever knelt to comfort a child as the tears flowed
down his or her little cheeks? If so, then you understand the
heart of your Daddy God as He gently wipes away your tears
during times of sorrow. He comforts as only a Father can,
bringing hope where there is no hope and joy where there is
no joy. What a compassionate God we serve!

Sorrows. . .Be Gone!

"I tell you the truth, you will weep
and mourn while the world rejoices.
You will grieve, but your grief will turn to joy."

JOHN 16:20 NIV

Imagine you're washing a load of white towels. One of them is badly stained. You add bleach to the wash load and let it run its cycle. Afterward, you can't tell which towel is which! The same is true when we allow God to wash away our sorrows. When all is said and done, all that remains is the joy!

Partakers of Joy

But rejoice that you participate in the
sufferings of Christ, so that you may be
overjoyed when his glory is revealed.

1 PETER 4:13 NIV

*E*ver feel like you've signed on for the suffering but not the joy? We are called to be partakers in Christ's sufferings. We wouldn't really know Him if we didn't walk in the valleys occasionally. But, praise God! We are also partakers in His glorious resurrection. We have the power of the cross to spur us on! The time has come to trade in those sorrows. Reach for His unspeakable joy.

A Deeper Joy

You changed my sorrow into dancing. You took away my
clothes of sadness, and clothed me in happiness.

PSALM 30:11 NCV

$\mathcal{S}$ometimes despair can feel like a deep well. You feel
trapped. Can't seem to find your way out to the daylight above.
Oh, friend! As deep as your well of sorrow might be, there is a
deeper joy. Finding it requires resting your head against the
Savior's chest, listening for His heartbeat until it beats in sync
with yours. Today, dig deep. . .and find that joy.

Temptation

Count It All Joy!

Consider it pure joy, my brothers,
whenever you face trials of many kinds.

JAMES 1:2 NIV

Temptations abound. We face them at every turn. On the television. In our conversations with friends. On the Internet. Today, as you contemplate the many temptations that life has to offer, count it all joy! The enemy knows we belong to the King of kings. That's the only reason he places stumbling blocks in our way. Next time he rears his ugly head, use joy as a weapon to fight him off.

Deliver Us. . .with Joy!

And lead us not into temptation, but deliver us from evil:
For thine is the kingdom, and the power,
and the glory, for ever. Amen.

MATTHEW 6:13 KJV

$\mathcal{H}$ave you ever been ensnared by the enemy? Led into
temptation? Caught in his trap? When you give your heart
to Christ, you are set free from your past, delivered from the
bondage of sin. Talk about a reason to celebrate. Nothing
is more glorious than being led out of a prison cell into the
sunlight. Oh, joyous freedom! Today, praise God for the things
He has delivered you from.

The Spirit Is Willing

"Watch and pray, lest you enter into temptation.
The spirit indeed is willing, but the flesh is weak."

MARK 14:38 NKJV

We've got to be on our guard for unexpected attacks.
Temptation can strike at any point. We might feel strong—
might convince ourselves we're not vulnerable—but our
flesh is weak! We often end up giving in, even when we're
determined not to. Today, ask the Lord to prepare you for any
temptations that might come your way. Then, with joy in your
heart, be on your guard!

A Joyous Crown

Blessed is the man who perseveres under trial, because
when he has stood the test, he will receive the crown of
life that God has promised to those who love him.

JAMES 1:12 NIV

$\mathcal{W}$e are so focused on the joys of this life that we
sometimes forget the exquisite joys yet to come in the next.
Enduring and overcoming temptation can bring us great
satisfaction here on earth, but imagine the crown of life we're
one day going to receive. Nothing can compare! Oh, the joy of
eternal life. Oh, the thrill of that joyous crown.

Rooted and Grounded

"Those on the rock are the ones who
receive the word with joy when they hear it,
but they have no root. They believe for a while,
but in the time of testing they fall away."

LUKE 8:13 NIV

Imagine a sturdy oak tree, one that's been growing for decades. Its roots run deep. It's grounded. When the storms of life strike, that tree is going to stand strong. Now think of your own roots. Do they run deep? When temptations strike, will you stand strong? Dig into the Word. Receive it with joy. Let it be your foundation. Plant yourself and let your roots run deep.

_____

_____

_____

_____

_____

_____

_____

_____

_____

_____

_____

Thankfulness

A Thankful Heart

Let the peace of Christ rule in your hearts,
since as members of one body you were
called to peace. And be thankful.

COLOSSIANS 3:15 NIV

$\mathcal{H}$ave you ever received really great news. . .unexpectedly?
Remember the inexplicable joy that rose up as you received it?
You didn't conjure it up; the joy came quite naturally. Today,
the news is good! God loves you! He cares for your needs
and surrounds you on every side. He is your defense. As you
contemplate these things, watch out! Joy is sure to fill your heart!

Hem Your Blessings

Everything God created is good,
and to be received with thanks.

I Timothy 4:4 MSG

Sometimes we walk through seasons of blessing and forget to be grateful. It's easy, with the busyness of life, to overlook the fact that Someone has made provision to cover the monthly bills. Someone has graced us with good health. Someone has given us friends and loved ones to share our joys and sorrows. Today, pause a moment, and thank the Lord for the many gifts He's poured out. Hem in those blessings!

....

....

....

....

....

....

....

....

....

....

....

Thanks. . .Again!

How can we thank God enough for you
in return for all the joy we have in the
presence of our God because of you?

I THESSALONIANS 3:9 NIV

Think of the people God has placed in your life—your family members, friends, co-workers, and other loved ones. They bring such joy and happiness to your life, don't they? Now contemplate this. . .what if you'd never met any of them? How different would your life be? These folks are such a gift! God has given them to you as a special present. . .one you need to remember to thank Him for.

Thanking Him. . .Publicly!

Give thanks unto the LORD,
call upon his name, make known
his deeds among the people.

I CHRONICLES 16:8 KJV

It's one thing to thank God in the privacy of your prayer closet; it's another to openly talk about the amazing things He's done in your life in front of a watching world. The words of your mouth, lifted up in joyful testimony, could have an amazing impact on those around you. So, go ahead. . .thank Him publicly. Share the things He's done with people you come in contact with. Make His deeds known!

Thanks Be to God!

I am grateful that God always makes it possible
for Christ to lead us to victory.

2 CORINTHIANS 2:14 CEV

God has created us to be victors, not victims. We are image-bearers of Christ and born to triumph! So, how do you see yourself today? Have you made up your mind to overcome in the areas where you've struggled? One way to assure your victory is to praise God for it. . .even before it happens. That's right! Praise your way through! Oh, the joy of triumphing in Christ!

187

Vision

A Royal Vision

Yes, joyful are those who live like this!
Joyful indeed are those whose God is the LORD.

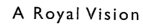

PSALM 144:15 NLT

$\mathcal{H}$ow wonderful to realize you're God's child. He loves you and wants nothing but good for you. Doesn't knowing you're His daughter send waves of joy through your soul? How happy we are when we recognize that we are princesses. . .children of the most high God! Listen closely as He whispers royal secrets in your ear. Your heavenly Father offers you keys to the Kingdom. . .and vision for the road ahead.

....

....

....

....

....

....

....

....

....

....

"Happy Is He. . ." (or She!)

Where there is no vision, the people perish:
but he that keepeth the law, happy is he.

PROVERBS 29:18 KJV

$\mathcal{E}$ver wish you could see into tomorrow? Wish you knew what was coming around the bend? While we can't see into the future, we can prepare for it by trusting God to bring us His very best. And while our "literal" vision can't glimpse the unseen tomorrow, we can prepare for it by staying close to the Lord and spending time in His Word. Peace and joy come when we trust God with our future!

A Joyous Stand

May he give you the desire of your heart
and make all your plans succeed. We will shout
for joy when you are victorious and will lift
up our banners in the name of our God.

PSALM 20:4–5 NIV

It's hard to have a vision for tomorrow if you're not excited
about today! Each day is a gift, after all, and an opportunity to
live for Christ. Today, take a stand for the things you believe
in. Lift high His name. Not only will you bring joy to His heart
(and your own), you will find yourself looking forward to a joy-
filled tomorrow.

_____

_____

_____

_____

_____

_____

_____

_____

_____

_____

_____

_____

_____

An Ear to Hear

He that hath an ear, let him hear what
the Spirit saith unto the churches.

REVELATION 2:17 KJV

We need to "lean in" to the Lord on a daily basis. Listen to His still, small voice. Catch a glimpse of His vision for the church. Ride on the wind of the Spirit. Today, as you draw close to the Lord, listen closely. What is He speaking into your life? May your joy be full as you "tune in" to the voice of the Holy Spirit.

Seeing the Invisible

Now faith is being sure of what we hope
for and certain of what we do not see.

HEBREWS 11:1 NIV

*Y*ou must look at your future as hopeful, and filled with wonderful "what ifs." No, you're not promised tomorrow. But if you give up on your hopes and dreams, if you lose sight of the plans the Lord has laid on your heart, they will surely not come to pass. Trust God to make the invisible. . .visible. And in the meantime, rejoice! You have a lot to look forward to!

....

....

....

....

....

....

....

....

....

....

....

Wisdom

Wisdom. . .What Joy!

Happy is the man who finds wisdom,
and the man who gains understanding.

PROVERBS 3:13 NKJV

*I*magine you've lost a priceless jewel—one passed down from your grandmother to your mother and then to you. You search everywhere, under every rock, in every closet. Still, you can't find it. Finally, in the least likely spot. . .you discover it! Joy floods your soul! Now imagine that "jewel" is wisdom. You've stumbled across it, and oh, what a treasure! Talk about a happy find!

The Key to Happiness

He who heeds the word wisely will find good,
and whoever trusts in the LORD, happy is he.

PROVERBS 16:20 NKJV

Want the key to true happiness? Try wisdom. When others around you are losing their heads, losing their cool, and losing sleep over their decisions, choose to react differently. Step up to the plate. Handle matters wisely. Wise choices always lead to joyous outcomes. And along the way, you will be setting an example for others around you to follow. So, c'mon. . .get happy! Get wisdom!

_____

_____

_____

_____

_____

_____

_____

_____

_____

_____

Walking Uprightly

Folly is joy to him who is destitute of discernment,
but a man of understanding walks uprightly.

PROVERBS 15:21 NKJV

Ever noticed that people who have something to hide don't
look others in the eye? Their gaze shifts up, down, and all
around. But those who walk uprightly can look others in the
eye without guilt or shame. Live wisely. Hold your head high.
Look folks in the eye. Let wisdom lead the way and watch as joy
follows!

Seek Out Wisdom

I applied mine heart to know, and
to search, and to seek out wisdom.

ECCLESIASTES 7:25 KJV

$\mathcal{R}$emember when you participated in your first Easter egg
hunt? You searched under every bush, every tree, until you
found one of those shiny eggs. The quest for wisdom is much
like that. You've got to look under a lot of shrubs to find it,
especially in this day and age. Oh, but what a prize! Today, as
you apply your heart to the Word of God, seek out wisdom.
What a joyous treasure!

_____

_____

_____

_____

_____

_____

_____

_____

_____

_____

The Words of My Mouth

She speaks with wisdom, and faithful
instruction is on her tongue.

PROVERBS 31:26 NIV

*H*ave you ever known someone who epitomized wisdom?
What set her apart from others of your acquaintance? A truly
wise person thinks carefully before speaking and only opens
her mouth when wisdom is ready to flow out. Kindness is on
her tongue. There's great joy in "becoming" wise in this way.
Today, guard your tongue! Think before you speak. By doing
so, you bring joy to others. . .and yourself.

197

Witness

A Net of Love

No one has ever seen God; but if we love one another,
God lives in us and his love is made complete in us.

1 JOHN 4:12 NIV

It's hard to be a good witness if you've got a sour expression on your face. People aren't usually won to the Lord by grumpy friends and co-workers. If you hope to persuade people that life in Jesus is the ultimate, then you've got to let your enthusiasm shine through. Before you reach for the net, spend some time on your knees, asking for an infusion of joy. Then, go catch some fish!

_____

_____

_____

_____

_____

_____

_____

_____

_____

_____

_____

A Witness to the Nations

"Go therefore and make disciples
of all the nations."

MATTHEW 28:19 NASB

*H*ave you ever pondered the mandate in Matthew's Gospel
to go into all the world and preach the gospel? Ever feel like
you're not doing your part? God calls us to be witnesses
where we are—to bloom where we're planted. Imagine the joy
of leading a neighbor or a friend to the Lord. So, instead of
fretting over not doing enough, delight in the fact that you are
usable. . .right where you are.

Powerful Witnesses

"But you will receive power when the Holy Spirit
has come upon you; and you shall be My witnesses
both in Jerusalem, and in all Judea and Samaria,
and even to the remotest part of the earth."

ACTS 1:8 NASB

$\mathcal{W}$ant to experience real joy in your life? Then become a powerful witness. The most effective witness for Christ is one who is wholly surrendered to God's will, and who has invited the Holy Spirit to do a transforming work in her life. After all, we can't really share the good news if our lives haven't been truly changed. Allow the Lord to renovate you from the inside out—then change your world!

Blooming for All to See

Since God chose you to be the holy people he loves,
you must clothe yourselves with tenderhearted mercy,
kindness, humility, gentleness, and patience.

COLOSSIANS 3:12 NLT

*H*ave you ever noticed that we're naturally drawn to people
who are fun to be around. . .people who radiate joy? They are
like a garden of thornless roses: They put off a beautiful aroma
and draw people quite naturally. If you want to win people
to the Lord, then woo them with your kindness. Put off an
inviting aroma. Win them with your love. Radiate joy!

Bearing Witness

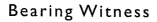

The life appeared; we have seen it and testify to it,
and we proclaim to you the eternal life,
which was with the Father and has appeared to us.

1 JOHN 1:2 NIV

$\mathcal{W}$e don't have to work hard at being good witnesses when we're walking in close relationship with the Lord. Our witness will flow quite naturally out of our relationship with God. In other words, we "are" witnesses, simply by living the life He's called us to live. And by living the life, we point others toward eternal life. Now, that will cause joy to rise up in your soul!

Work

Not Withholding

Anything I wanted, I would take. I denied myself
no pleasure. I even found great pleasure in
hard work, a reward for all my labors.

ECCLESIASTES 2:10 NLT

Work beckons. Deadlines loom. You're trying to balance your home life against your work life, and it's overwhelming. Take heart! It is possible to rejoice in your labors—to find pleasure in the day-to-day tasks. At work or at play. . .let the Lord cause a song of joy to rise up in your heart.

Joy in Your Work

Go, eat your food with gladness, and drink
your wine with a joyful heart, for it is
now that God favors what you do.

ECCLESIASTES 9:7 NIV

*E*ver feel like nothing you do is good enough? Your boss
is frustrated over something you've done wrong. The kids
are complaining. Your neighbors are even upset at you. How
wonderful to read that God accepts our works, even when
we feel lacking. He encourages us to go our way with a merry
heart, completely confident that we are accepted in the
Beloved.

....

....

....

....

....

....

....

....

....

....

Joyous Petitions

Delight yourself in the LORD and he
will give you the desires of your heart.

PSALM 37:4 NIV

*W*hat are the deepest desires of your heart? Ponder that question a moment. If you could really do—or have—what you longed for, what would that be? The key to receiving from the Lord is delighting in Him. Draw near. Spend time with your head against His shoulder, feeling His heartbeat. Ask that your requests come into alignment with His will. Then, with utmost joy, make your petitions known.

The Fork in the Road

What does a man get for all the
toil and anxious striving with
which he labors under the sun?

ECCLESIASTES 2:22 NIV

*I*magine you're approaching a fork in the road. You're unsure of which way to turn. If you knew ahead of time that the road to the right would be filled with joy and the road to left would lead to sorrow, wouldn't it make the decision easier? Today, as you face multiple decisions, ask God to lead you down the right road.

_____

_____

_____

_____

_____

_____

_____

_____

_____

_____

The Fruit of Your Labor

You will eat the fruit of your labor;
blessings and prosperity will be yours.

PSALM 128:2 NIV

$\mathcal{W}$e're always waiting for the payoff, aren't we? When we've put a lot of effort into a project, for example, we hope to see good results. The Word of God promises that we will eat the fruit of our labor—that we will eventually experience blessings and prosperity. So, all that hard work will be worth it. But remember, the joy is in the journey! It's not just in the payoff.

Scripture Index

Old Testament

Proverbs

Ecclesiastes

Isaiah

Lamentations

New Testament

Romans

1 Corinthians

Colossians

1 Thessalonians

1 Timothy

2 Timothy

Titus

Philemon

Hebrews

James

1 Peter